MW00593435

Dear Deb,

We hope you enjoy reading about all of our pug adventures!

And, well, when Mom was really a rookie at all of this pug stuff.

With lots of pug hugs,

Zoe

+

Jennifer

The Grumbly Pug

Life & Love with Zoe

Jennifer
Niland
Wright

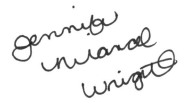

AUTHOR™
& COMPANY

Connecticut • New York • Colorado

THE GRUMBLY PUG
LIFE AND LOVE WITH ZOE

Zoe drawing by Lisa Mary Secundo

This book was designed by iLN™
and manufactured in the United States of America.

"This sweetheart and spitfire of a lady has raised some amazing pugs and husbands. She has given me both of the best. To Gail and Michael, I would not have these stories if not for you. I love you to pieces."

A portion of the proceeds of this book will be donated to two organizations very special to us.

National Mill Dog Rescue (NMDR) strives to save all of the Coley's of the world. NMDR rescues, rehabilitates and re-homes discarded breeding dogs. Please learn more at milldogrescue.org.

The NAZ Children's Centre, located in Rose Hall, Jamaica, serves children from kindergarten through grade six in a holistic learning environment. Funded largely by donations, the NAZ Centre encourages children with and without disabilities to work at their optimum while learning from their families, teachers, and each other in a setting that does not discriminate. Please visit them at nazchildrenscentre.com.

CONTENTS

The Grumbly Pug

CONTENTS

I know what you're thinking. The scarf is borderline clothes, which is a sore subject that you will soon learn more about.

Well, my friend, I let this one slide. Mom had been sick. So, Michael and I decided that I should wear a cute little scarf to cheer her up. Anything (almost) for my Mom.

INTRODUCTION

"**B**ecause I'm awesome. Obviously."

This was Zoe's response when I asked her why someone would want to buy her book. This answer came swiftly, enthusiastically, and without hesitation. Of course. My eighteen-pound stubborn, curly tailed, wrinkly faced little pug has more confidence in one of her grey whiskers than I could hope to have in my forty years. Life doesn't come easy to her; rather she *makes* it that way, through sheer will and refusal to accept anything less. Why would her approach to the publishing world be any different?

Knowing that I needed to come up with something more than her self-declaration of awesomeness, I started to reflect back on our life together. I don't think of it as our lives in the plural, rather it's a singular life, because our hearts and minds are woven together in one interchangeable bank of memories. As we have both aged, I have come to realize that there is common thread throughout those memories. That thread is Zoe's voice.

You see, no matter the situation, Zoe has the confidence of self to speak out and speak up, even when I, myself, hesitate to do so. Through the years, this voice has earned her a reputation. We were not invited back to the barn after she bit my friend Liz's horse on the nose. Then there was the tollbooth incident. And the ladies at the vet came to call her the "other" one, as that was the nicest adjective they could collectively think of. It's not that Zoe is mean to anyone on purpose. She just doesn't need the validation of a stranger's pat on her head to know that she is fantastic.

Zoe is my calm when life storms and my giggling best friend when we share an inside joke. What better way to honor that voice than to share it with the world? Because, in the end, I know that's exactly what Zoe would tell me to do.

So my friends, I hope you enjoy this small (but large, if you know what I mean) collection of love and laughter from my dear Zoe, the grumbliest little pug on the planet.

The Grumbly Pug

Life & Love with Zoe

Running

I did it once. On the beach. For two minutes. (Yes, I am still talking about running. This book is PG, my friend.)

You may ask, "Zoe, you look like you were having fun, why didn't you run again?" I submit to you the answer to that fine question. Exhibit A.

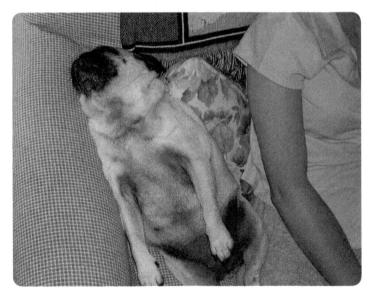

Exhibit A: *A self-portrait I like to call "Evening After Running".*

Sink or Swim

When I was about two years old, I learned the truth. I'm a sinker not a swimmer.

Mom and I were so happy before the big event.

This dramatic story started at Grandpa Rick's house. Grandpa Rick is Michael's dad and was married to Grandma Gail a long, long, *long* time ago. (Hard to imagine those two together. What in the world was she thinking? Oh, sorry Mom, I'll get back to the story.) Grandpa Rick and I have a love/hate relationship. He hates me because I'm a pug. And I love peeing on his ottoman.

On this fateful summer day we were all sitting around Grandpa Rick's gleaming new swimming pool when Michael warned Mom – "Watch Zoe, she may try to jump in." Mom replied, "Yeah, right, she's smarter than that." Well, my friends, I wasn't smarter than that. I figured I could tip toe into the sparkling blue water, get my feet a little wet, and then safely run back to shore, just like I do on the beach in Maine. I have bravely dodged the imposing waves of the great Atlantic; this miniature ocean full of foam noodles didn't scare me! So I took one slow step off the edge and "whoomp", the chilly water immediately engulfed me, and I sunk like an adorable, quick witted, 18-pound *rock*. My over-privileged life flashed before my eyes.

I then heard a second, even larger "whoomp". Just when I thought I could paddle no longer I felt Michael's arm around me, and we quickly ascended to the surface. My hero had jumped in right after me, in all of his clothes, to ensure my rescue! As he placed me on the pool deck, I heard him mutter something like "I told you so" to Mom and "these shoes *were* brand new." Mom did not respond. She was frozen at the sight of my waterlogged body. She quickly wrapped me in a fuzzy, warm beach towel and hugged me harder than I had ever felt before.

While the whole family was cuddling me and offering me hot dogs upon my safe return, I heard Grandpa Rick say "Great, a *dog* ruined my clean pool, I better not have any dog fur in my new filters". I looked at him and smiled. Not to worry, no fur Grandpa Rick, but I'm pretty sure I peed a little bit.

Santa

S anta Claus. Hmm. This is a touchy subject for me.

On the one hand, he brings me some great stuff on Christmas morning. On the other hand, my Mom makes me sit on his lap on Christmas Eve. And it's really weird because he looks oddly like my cousin Kyle, which sort of freaks me out. All of my family exclaims, "Oh Zoe looks so cute on Santa's lap!" Does Santa have a biscuit for me? Nope. A piece of cheese? Nope. A deviled egg? You guessed it, nope. I fail to see what's in it for me on his Christmas Eve visit.

In this picture I'm 25 in dog years. Cleary too old for Santa's lap. Heck, at this age I could drive, vote, drink, and join the Army. ("Zoe, are you sure about that?" you're probably asking. OK, well, maybe not the Army. They'd try to push me out of the helicopter to get the bad guy and I'd be like "Um, wait, I didn't get my complimentary peanuts yet! Do you see how high we are? How do *I* know the parachute will open? The German Shepherd Dog over there looks like he *really* wants to do it!")

"Okay fine, Zoe," you may say, "Christmas Eve doesn't work out but certainly you must score on Christmas Day with the big family you have!" A big fat nope, my friend! Christmas Day, when we go to Grandma Gail's, all of the grandchildren open mountains of gifts. Do the aunts and uncles get me presents? You see where this is going. Big fat nope! Do I not count because I have fur; lack opposable thumbs, and may need to brush up on my table manners?

But Zoe, you might press, "Aren't you missing the point of the Christmas Spirit?" Nope! As far as I'm concerned the Christmas Spirit is about looking out for the ones you love. I love myself and, I suffer.

Exception: *My Aunt Fran always buys me Christmas presents. And they are usually edible. The best kind! She's my favorite. Oh, and because she's my favorite, I'm putting her picture in my book. Just because I can.*

Siblings

O kay, so up to this point, I think you've assumed that I have always been an only child. Technically I wasn't an only child when Michael and Mom brought me home. They had a lop-eared bunny rabbit. So, I had a brother from another mother. (I'm so glad Mom lets me watch Kevin Hart movies).

Our first Christmas together.

Let's just say this rabbit was pretty dumb. You know, not the smartest bunny in the hutch. "Wow, Zoe," you may be saying to yourself, "dumb is a bit harsh." Fine, but when's the last time you saw a dog fall in the toilet? That's what I thought.

Puts the lid on *that* argument, right? (If you have a rabbit, you may need to explain that joke to him.)

This rabbit's name was Thurman. Michael said they named him after a very famous New York Yankee. So naturally, I asked, "What famous and fabulous person was I named after?" Michael told me I wasn't named after anyone, confirming my theory that I'm famous and fabulous all by myself. Oh, sorry, sort of drifted, back to my story about Thurman.

While we made for some pretty fantastic Christmas cards, my relationship with Thurman was not one you would call deep and meaningful.

Anyways, I tried to work on my relationship with Thurman, but it developed something like this:

Me as a Puppy:
I want to play!

Thurman:
Um, what the heck are you doing?

(Mom may have edited out his salty language. Yep, this rabbit used salty language)

Go away!

Me as a Puppy:
It's cold out!
Let's cuddle!

Thurman:
Um, what the hell
are you doing?
Go away!

Me 3 Months Older:
I AM BIGGER THAN
YOU NOW. I want
to play! Now!

Thurman:
Um, I don't care.
You can't make me
be your friend.
Go away!

Thurman: *Hey Zoe, do you know what a German Shepherd Dog is?*

Me: *Nope.*

Thurman: *Karma!*

(Mom says this joke of Thurman's is called dramatic fore-shadowing to keep you, dear reader, hooked. Is it working?)

Mom's Car

For my male readers, I'd like to offer a word of advice: at some point in your marriage, you should really buy your wife a car, as a *gift*, and better yet, as a *surprise*. Now I know what you're thinking "Zoe, I can't just go out and drop thousands of dollars on a car for my wife." Okay, fine, but at the very minimum you can consider an attractive lease offer.

Mom, me and her pug bug.

After two years of marriage (aka, when my parents still didn't know what the heck they were doing) Michael decided to surprise Mom with her dream car. A 2001 VW "New Beetle". Now, this was my Mom's dream car, but she was also cheap (sorry Mom, I meant "frugal") and did not want to spend the money on a cute little Volkswagen.

Up to that point, while Mom was dreaming about a little VW, Michael and she would visit the VW dealership on Sunday afternoons (when they were closed) so Mom could drool all over the cute little Beetles in relative privacy.

After *months* of Sunday afternoon visits to VW, Michael secretly decided he was going to "buy Mom the darn car already" (his words, not mine, you know I don't like to use that type of salty language).

So that following Tuesday, Michael asked Mom to switch cars. Mom was puzzled by this request because normally she couldn't peel his Chevy Blazer keys out of his clenched freckled hands. Michael explained that he was going to get her car detailed for her. Mom was pleased as punch that Michael cared so much about her little green Mazda.

See, my friends, to say my Mom is a bit obsessive-compulsive about keeping her car clean is being polite. In her family, you buy Walmart floor mats to put over your "good" floor mats that come with the car. You can't get the "good" floor mats dirty! And when it comes to keeping that car clean, you happily spend three hours on a Saturday afternoon at the local do-it-yourself car wash. You don't let *some stranger* wash your car. You scrub, vacuum, foam, and polish all by yourself, tearing through rolls of quarters. And, if you get to go to the car wash in our neighborhood, you can listen to the happiest sounding salsa music. Hey, I'm starting to learn a mean cha-cha! (Wish I could say the same for Mom.)

Sorry, back to the story. So, little did Mom know, yes,

Michael was having her car detailed, but he was doing it to *trade it in for the New Beetle.* He completed the deal in less than two hours. The only thing Michael couldn't do was the final paperwork on Mom's Mazda as it was in her name. Apparently Volkswagen of Meriden frowns upon accepting a trade-in on a car the owner *doesn't know is being sold.* Michael got a great deal for the trade in. (No doubt because of the pristine "good" floor mats.)

With this little trade-in wrinkle, Michael moved on to phase two of his plan. Michael and Mom followed their same VW drooling routine the next Sunday. They brought me this time, because after VW, we were going to Grandma Gail's for Sunday dinner. (I was not going to miss out on her meatloaf and mashed potatoes.) When we arrived at VW, Mom did her normal scan of all of the New Beetles, dreaming about which one she would buy someday. *Maybe. Possibly.* Mom is nothing if not decisive. (Insert sarcastic cough here.)

Mom raced over to a navy blue Beetle and declared it was the perfect one. Well, Michael had already *bought* Mom's car, and that navy blue Beetle definitely was not it. His heart sank. Michael then quickly regrouped and directed Mom to the bright yellow Beetle parked in the corner of the lot. Mom and I ran (okay, fine, Mom carried me) over to it. Mom looked it over and yelled back to Michael, "It's lovely, but did you see the price? Who in their right mind would spend that much money on a car?!?" Michael, that's who. And his heart sank a second time.

But, not one to give up easily, Michael pointed out all

of the car's features, giving his best sales pitch. Mom and her wallet weren't budging. So Michael finally caved, this surprise wasn't going exactly according to script. "Jen, did you look in the front window of the yellow car?" As mom had been scrutinizing the car's invoice, she neglected to notice that her NAME and SOLD were in huge grey letters were scrawled across the front windshield. Michael went on, "*Now* do you like the yellow one? Happy Birthday?!?!" As those words came stumbling out of Michael's mouth, Mom's frugality flew out the power sunroof. She jumped up and hugged her shiny new yellow car. Then she hugged Michael. Then me. I'm so glad I was there that day. The look on my Mom's face was one I will never forget. It was sheer joy. Michael did something for Mom that she, in a million years, would never have done for herself. It no longer was just about the car. And, in that moment, we all knew that.

As for me, I got to cruise the town in a sweet ride in the *front* seat for the first time ever. See, the real beauty of the VW Beetle was that my crate was too big for the back seat. One point for Zoe! And, Mom got a license plate befitting of such a cool, cute and yellow car. She requested our new personal plate from the Connecticut DMV, and in a few weeks (I guess it takes the inmates in the clink a while to pound those things out), we were driving our little yellow "ZOE PUG" around town.

Michael has since bought Mom another car, replacing the Beetle. Once a few New England winters rolled past, you see, we realized the cute little yellow Beetle wasn't so cute when Michael had to rescue Mom from two inches of snow in the

Aetna parking lot. And while Mom has kept her "ZOE PUG" license plate, she has tossed her frugality aside for increasingly finer German engineering. She insists it's not about the car really, but rather that we are always driving surrounded by Michael's love. And yes, she still puts Walmart floor mats over the good ones.

Cousins

M ichael has a lot of brothers and sisters so therefore I have a boatload of human cousins. I especially love my little cousins. They are closer to the ground for hugs and they tend to drop a lot food. You can keep the Cheerios but Goldfish crackers are delicious!

Bust number one!

Oh, and their fingers are perpetually sticky and consistently tasty. The only drawback to cousins? They blame their farts on me. But my cousin Ricky always gets busted. On this vacation in Maine...twice!

And bust number two!

Christmas Cards

So friends, we trust each other pretty well by now, right? Then, here goes.

I'm pretty happy that Mom and Michael don't have any non-furry children. This lets them pour all of their love, time and nurturing energy into me.

This sweetest of deals comes with one hitch. Christmas cards. Bah humbug.

Right after this picture was taken, Mom took away the plate of chocolate chip cookies and I dove for the milk.

Ugh! Puppies! Get me out of here!

Photo Ops

I'm not trying to be braggy or anything, but I really was an exceptional puppy. While my littermates were nice and all, they were, well… dogs. I was Zoe. Guess which one I am in this picture? While most of them were all sleepy and snorey, sprawled out in our bed, clearly not showing their best sides, I saw a camera, and I was ready. Mom says my face was all, "I'm cute and sweet," but I was more like "Help! Get me out of here!"

Does this bench make my butt look fat?

*As Irresistible
Puppy Prisoner*

*Hanging out with
my jet ski.*

Rescue

I didn't' learn what the word "rescue" truly meant until I was seven years old. As far as I was concerned, rescue was firemen and the Coast Guard. Like me, I thought, all dogs got wonderful families, and unless there was a fire, flood, or shortage of bacon, they didn't need to be "rescued" from

*My little
sad Coley.*

anything. Sadly, it turns out, many dogs aren't as lucky as I am. For some reason (and I rack my brain trying to figure it out) their humans don't treat them well and some don't even love them. So, kind-hearted humans rescue these dogs from the bad people and find them new homes with the good people. There these dogs can be loved. Their rescue families can cuddle with them on the couch, feed them good meals, give them lots of toys, sleep with them in a warm bed, and show them the wonderful life of a well-loved dog.

My sister Coley was one of these dogs who needed rescue. I dedicate this chapter to her rescue angel, Samantha, who made it possible for Coley to leave her life with the bad people and find a new home with us, the good people.

And yes, it's a long chapter, but Coley's story deserves to not be rushed.

Sometimes rescues can be like they sound, very dramatic, and Coley's rescue fit the bill. The details are sketchy, but from what I know, Coley was one of four pugs that belonged to a woman who lived in Yonkers, NY. Yonkers lady was moving and supposedly could only take one pug with her. She called the rescue group on *Christmas Eve* and said that if someone didn't come ASAP to take the three remaining pugs, she would leave them behind, in the empty apartment in the middle of winter, to fend for themselves. One of her pugs was 10 years old and she considered just putting him to sleep, for convenience. I have a few choice words for Yonkers lady. Should I ever meet her in a dark alley, she would be on the business end of my 12 remaining teeth. (Sorry, I went on a tangent there, but things like this rattle me.)

Well, as it turns out, one of the Yonkers lady pugs was a four-year-old female, who was pregnant, and Samantha would be her rescuer. Samantha was not told how far along in pregnancy this pug was or any details about her health. Any good "breeder" (and I use this term very loosely here) knows that dogs are pregnant for 63 days, so you count the days from when… yada, yada, yada, and ta da! You get a due date. Or at least a range. Turns out this not-sure-how-pregnant female was named "Colesta" by Yonkers-lady, who not only was horrible to dogs, but rotten at math, and terrible with names. Colesta? Really? (It sounds like a drug for clogged arteries.) Well, upon rescue, one of the first things Samantha did to give this little pug a new start was to bless her with a new name, Coley. Unusual, but pretty. Sort of like this little dog.

Others from Samantha's group rescued the other Yonkers pugs. The 10-year-old was not put to sleep; he went to live with a family in Manhattan and went on to enjoy life in the Big Apple.

Upon rescue, Samantha and her mom officially took responsibility for Coley, becoming her foster parents. They rushed to the store to buy supplies for her, as Coley came with NOTHING. Not even a collar or leash. And, as it was Christmas Eve, they bought doggy Christmas presents including a blanket and toys. But Coley didn't know what to do with them. She had never had them before. Samantha would later tell me how scared Coley was that night. Wouldn't you be? So far in Coley's life, all people were mean to her. Why would she think Samantha and her mom would be any different?

For the next few weeks, Samantha and her family showered Coley with love. The timid little dog slowly emerged from her shell, settling in to her nice new life as her belly continued to swell. Samantha took Coley to her veterinarian, the jolly Dr. Hexter, for some much needed medical care. Dr. Hexter treated Coley for a fraction of the normal costs, as he has such a big heart, and he guessed that Coley hadn't had much, if any, veterinary care in the past. Dr. Hexter estimated Coley's due date based on her condition and belly size. As her due date was fast approaching, Samantha combed through her "dog-people" connections to find a breeder to help. They needed a kind, experienced breeder to "whelp" Coley's puppies. Coley needed special care. They also needed a breeder who would have the knowledge, time, and heart to take care of Coley and her puppies around the clock for eight weeks. An expert was also important, as the lack of early (or any) veterinary care made Coley and her puppies medically fragile. It's amazing all of the things that can go wrong when a healthy, well cared for dog gives birth, so for a dog like Coley, everything was high-risk.

Grandma Gail's puppy room

As luck would have it, Samantha tracked down my Grandma Gail! At that time, Grandma Gail had been breeding pugs for 30 years, well before America fell in love with Frank from *Men In Black*. Arrangements quickly made, Coley soon found herself in the home and the arms of Grandma Gail. They had no idea how many puppies were to be born; they could not put Coley through the stress of an ultrasound. They didn't know if the puppies were healthy, if they were pugs, or if they were even alive. Stillborn puppies happen to even the best of breeders and healthiest of dogs, so it was a real concern for Coley's little ones.

Grandma Gail's puppy room became Coley's new home. Yes, Grandma Gail has a special doggy nursery. It's decorated with custom-made pug curtains and matching bedding. It is stocked with puppy cribs, puppy scales, puppy formula, blankets, heat lamps, and metal clampy things that when I inquired Mom just said, "Don't ask". Oh, and it's also temperature, germ, and access controlled.

See, Grandma Gail requires you to show photo ID and proof of immunizations before she'll let you through the door. OK, maybe I'm exaggerating on the photo ID, but she does make you "scrub in". And, until they're five weeks old, with their immune systems more strongly established, you CANNOT TOUCH A PUPPY. Grandma Gail will happily talk to you about the puppies and show you the puppies. If you value all of your fingers and toes, *you will not touch a puppy*. She looks all cute, sweet, Irish grandmother here, but if you mess with her dogs, Grandma Gail will hurt you.

Sorry, back to Coley. After one week of basking in Grandma Gail's pre-natal comforts, on a cold January night, Coley began signs of labor. Her temperature dropped. She began to pant. She started circling and digging up the layers of blankets in the corners of her pen. Literally, nesting.

Later that night Coley gave birth to three healthy, beautiful, perfect pug puppies. And, even better, Coley had no complications. Grandma Gail quickly saw she was a wonderful mom! Coley gently fed and cleaned her pups, lovingly watched over them, protectively growling if another pug got too close to her pen, and kept them all warm without smothering them (which, while it sounds obvious, is not always a given). See, not all pugs are good moms. Mine, for example, took one look at my five siblings and me and promptly jumped out of our pen, and with her two bulgy brown eyes glaring at Grandma Gail, declared, "You did this to me. I didn't ask for them. They're all yours!" And off she went. But not Coley, she was perfect. Grandma Gail gathered that she likely had many litters of puppies before, judging by her skilled mothering, prematurely worn body and overly swollen belly after birth.

As Grandma Gail spent more time with Coley she started to put the pieces together of Coley's earlier life, sort of like a detective. Coley likely had lived most of her life in a metal crate with a grate for a floor, as her paws where permanently splayed apart, like she spent her days trying to keep her balance on a series of tight ropes so as not to fall over in her crate. When Grandma Gail took her outside, it was as if grass was new to her, she tippy toed across each frozen blade,

Coley and her one-week-old puppies. She knew she was safe at Grandma Gail's.

lifting one paw at a time, to be prepared to potentially sink at any moment. She had a one-inch scar on her right hind side (you can see it in the picture), likely from a deep gash, never stitched, the origin remaining a mystery. And, her toenails were so long they were curling under, making it painful for her to walk. Two toenails on her back paws had actually grown into the pads of her feet, something even occasional toenail clippings would have helped to prevent. The pads themselves were dried and cracked, likely from dirty conditions and lack of a soft surface to sit or stand on. And even after several washings, Coley still smelled of the years of neglected baths and brushings. Clearly, Coley had not lived a nice life.

When the puppies were about a week old Grandma Gail deemed it safe for "external, blood-related visitors" to visit. I'm not kidding about blood-related. I can't count the times she's turned away potential, wide-eyed puppy visitors just so excited to get a glimpse of the little balls of fur. She's even banished her own grandchildren. Kids are FULL of germs! So with the formal OK, Michael and Mom (armed with their above mentioned photo IDs, vaccination records, and antimicrobial soap) raced over to meet Coley and the pups. Before they gingerly entered the puppy room, Grandma Gail warned, "Now, don't be too surprised guys, but Coley is a funny looking pug. She's got a bit of a snout, skinny legs, and a weirdly colored coat."

Coley and her six week old puppies.
She loved being a mom.

Now before you get all judgy about Grandma Gail picking on Coley's looks, you have to understand that

Grandma Gail has bred and raised some very perfect champion show dogs. Her prodigies have won ribbons all across the U.S. and Canada, including the prestigious Westminster Dog Show. This grand event is where the best 2,000 dogs from around the world descend on New York City's Madison Square Garden each February to compete for the coveted title of "Best in Show". Grandma Gail can pick apart a seemingly perfect dog, noting flaws not normally seen by the human eye. But that technical expertise is in no way a reflection of her undying love for all dogs. No matter what they look like. And, in this case, especially her love for Coley.

As I'm a professional cuddler, Coley learned quickly.

So as Michael and Mom peered into the puppy room to gaze at this "imperfect" dog, they immediately fell perfectly in love. And that was it. There was no question where Coley was spending the rest of her life. With us.

First Night with Coley

Coley's first night home with us was the last Friday in March. It was Michael's busy time at work, so it was just Mom, Coley and me. As Coley was still technically being taken care of by Grandma Gail and the pug rescue, the plan was for this arrangement to be a "trial weekend". Mom was to pick up Coley on Friday night and return her to Grandma Gail on Sunday evening.

Mom picked Coley up at Grandma Gail's after work, gathered up Coley's favorite blanket, and arrived home with my possible sister-to-be just after dark. I took one look at

Coley and my once selfish heart broke. Just like what Mom said, it was love at first sight. Coley would come to have that effect on just about everyone she met, furry or otherwise. I could see Coley's big brown eyes were full of worry. At that moment, I vowed it was my job to fix it. I would pull her out of her sad shell.

But first I told Coley about the practical stuff. I told her Mom is a hugger. That she feeds us tasty meals and delicious snacks. That she lets us finish her yogurt and lick the bowl when she bakes a cake (vanilla). We sleep in Mom's big bed with an electric blanket. We get lots of toys. We go to Dairy Queen for ice cream on warm (but not too warm for a pug) summer days. We play outside in the grass. We go to the park to chase the ducks and try not to get yelled at for eating their bread. We lie on the deck in the sunshine. After I explained all of this I thought for sure Coley would catch on, that life would be good. But she just gazed back at me with those sad, utterly confused brown eyes. My job was going to be harder than I thought.

Once she got Coley's things settled inside, Mom took us out to show Coley our nice big yard. I remember it was a warm evening for March in Connecticut, so we got to take our time. Mom put a leash on Coley and attached it to her bubble gum pink collar, as she wasn't sure if this frightened little pug would try to run away. It took Mom and me about 30 seconds to realize that was silly. Coley wasn't going anywhere. She maintained a distance of about six inches away from us, at all times. So Mom unclipped the nylon tether. Coley froze. It was like she was so panicked she was even too panicked to show us how panicked she was. So, to see what would happen, Mom took one small, gentle step forward. Coley took one equally small, tentative step forward. Mom to the left. Coley to the left. Mom to the right. Coley to the right. Time stood still in this sweet little dance. It was at that very moment that Mom became the sun to Coley's lost planet. From this second forward, Coley's life was to orbit, safely, around Mom's.

So with that progress, we got down to business. Literally. I showed Coley some of my favorite spots to potty. She moved slowly, but she caught on quickly. Clearly, she was not familiar with the joy of going potty outside. Instead, she had spent much of her life having to potty in her own cage, likely soiling herself. Mom wanted to reward Coley immediately, as she quickly picked up this new way to potty. Mom slowly bent down to say "good girl" and pat her on her little warm head. Coley flinched at Mom's touch. But Mom continued and spoke sweetly to her.

It worked like a charm! Upon hearing Mom's almost whisper soft, soothing words, Coley's ears retreated from the back of her head and her tail sprung up from between her legs to brush her back in a perfect, confident pug curl.

With the outside potty a success, Mom decided we should make it an early night. It had been a long day for all of us. Once back in the house, we quickly learned Coley was terribly afraid of the stairs. We tried our best to coax her, even just up one step, but her constant trembling and worried brow told us stairs might just not be for her. At least not for tonight. Stairs weren't for me either anymore, so I wasn't one to judge. I was seven years old and had decided that if my dog food said "senior" I was perfectly entitled to be carried up the stairs, regardless of my actual *ability* to climb them myself. I demanded, "carry me" and Coley's bulging eyes could not have screamed, "carry me" more loudly. So that's what Mom did. Pug under each arm.

Once upstairs Mom quickly changed into her jammies. (She said you could still call them "jammies"). She then scooped us up and clumsily plopped our combined 30 pounds of pug on her soft bed. I quickly settled into my spot on Mom's pillow. Coley stood at the foot of the bed, scared and perplexed. Mom and I tried to reassure her that this was a safe, comfy, warm place to settle in for the night. We gathered this was the first time Coley had sat on a real bed.

After about 30 minutes of gentle coaxing, Coley finally curled up in a spot in the crook of Mom's legs. She made sure she was close to us, but not too close. I was relieved and happy she finally settled in. I licked her ears a few times for reassurance and dove into my next position, tucked under Mom's left arm.

Mom and I woke up several times that night to keep a sort of half-sleep vigil over our new addition. We didn't know if Coley would get scared, have to go potty, get confused, or fall off the bed. We worried for no reason. Coley slept a heavy, solid sleep. She slept as if a weight was forever lifted. She slept with a full belly, in a warm bed, and beside a family that loved her.

That night was the first night of the rest of our lives with Coley. Mom never returned Coley to Grandma Gail's and secured her adoption with Samantha's rescue group that Monday morning.

They say that you cannot change the world by rescuing one dog, but for that one dog you forever change her entire world. The way I see it, we changed Coley's world, but she would come to change ours even more.

Parents

Brace yourself for the truth. Are you sitting down? All dogs are adopted! Once I got over the initial shock of this news, it started to make some sense. My birth mother couldn't cook, drive, or keep a tidy house. I don't think anyone would have hired her for an actual job. It's hard to type a resume without fingers and thumbs.

I guess it turns out well that humans become our parents. I got pretty lucky with mine. Grandma Gail is my biological mom's Mom. Her name is Franny (technically, Francesca

My parents and me!

Rose, beautiful, I know). Well anyways, Franny was pregnant with her first (and what would be her only) litter of puppies. This litter included, yes me, fabulous Zoe. My name was inspired by a song that Lenny Kravitz wrote for his baby daughter. The song is called "Flowers for Zoe", which is my official American Kennel Club name. The song itself is actually quite awful (sorry Lenny), but the sentiment is there.

Franny went into labor on a cold Friday night in the middle of January. Michael served as Grandma Gail's midwife when puppies were born. I'll spare you the gross details, but pugs need more help when they are giving birth as they have no snouts and have trouble opening and cleaning the individual gooey sacs that each puppy is born in. Oops, sorry, I didn't spare much detail there, did I? So when they got the call, Mom and Michael raced over to Grandma Gail's. I'm still a bit bothered that they showed up in their snow boots and flannel pajamas. I mean, didn't they know *I* was about to be born!

As Franny labored through the night, Michael helped Grandma Gail with each puppy. One at a time, about a half hour apart, three black boys were born. Then one fawn female. And so, three hours and four healthy puppies later, Franny, exhausted from the ordeal, began to rest. Grandma Gail surmised she was done. Pugs usually have small litters and Franny's four made for a nicely sized one. Then something happened, another puppy was coming! It was number five, a fawn female! Franny rested again, completely spent and thoroughly annoyed. Okay, she was *really* done this time. Grandma Gail started to settle the puppies in and clean

Franny up. Midnight passed. Everyone was tired. But wait, Franny got antsy again and twenty minutes later, another puppy! Number six! A breathtakingly gorgeous fawn female. *Hello world, it's ME, Zoe!* Of course I waited until after midnight. Why would I want to share my birthday with a bunch of dogs?!??!

Grandma Gail carefully examined all of us and declared us all healthy. It was determined that I had the one "fault" of the litter, which would mean I wasn't made for life as a show dog. I was born with a flat chest. I was still perfectly healthy but I "veered from the breed standard" for a Pug. But that flat chest would be my ticket out of life of working a show-ring to a glorious life of snoring on a couch and sleeping under the covers!

Mom and Michael immediately asked Grandma Gail if they could be my parents. Grandma Gail said she had to think about it. Think about it?!?! Michael is her cherished youngest son, the apple of her eye! As it turned out, Grandma Gail was reluctant to let me live with Mom and Michael because at the time they lived in an apartment. Grandma Gail wanted me to spend mornings playing in the dewy grass and afternoons lounging under shady trees. So Mom and Michael did what anyone in that situation would have done. They bought me a house.

In the end, I know I'm pretty lucky to have the human parents that I do. They give me a life to which I've grown accustomed. In return, I've given them – me.

Why Pugs Don't Pee in the Rain

I f you have a pug, you already know this, but for the rest of you sad pugless folks, I thought I'd help you out. (Mom says I have to be more "selfless".)

So, here goes, just a few reasons why pugs don't pee in the rain. Consider this an educational chapter.

1. It's wet. (Duh.)

2. It's usually cold. (We're stuck in Connecticut while Grandma Gail jets off to Florida in the winters.)

3. The ground is all mushy, and it just gives me heebie-jeebies. (Who *knows* what I'm stepping in?)

4. I no longer fit in my raincoat. (Don't ask.)

5. It makes my paws smell like mud. (I like when they smell like Downy.)

6. If I want to pee into something soft, I'll pee on the rug. (I may get yelled at, but I won't get wet.)

7. Mom doesn't carry me back inside because she says I'll get her wet. (Refer to item 1. Not my fault.)

8. Rain smells gross. (Remember dogs' noses are like a zillion times more sensitive than humans.)

9. I don't like to slip when I squat. (My knees aren't what they used to be.)

10. Mom usually gives me a bath because I smell "like wet dog" after we go out. (I usually respond, "Well, who else am I supposed to smell like when I'm wet?" That doesn't get me too far.)

There, done. Now off to find Mom so I can get the piece of cheese she promised me for being selfless.

Self-Control

Listen carefully, for if you remember nothing else from this book, please remember this – self-control is overrated. If you have an opportunity (hypothetically, of course) to grab some crumbs from under the kitchen sink when Mom's not looking, *go for it!* Just put on your innocent face, and you're home free.

Here I am under the kitchen sink. In my house, it's a crumb filled bonanza!

Maybe face down into a
bowl of cake batter is
more your speed.

Have at it!

Say there's a big
picnic, and you
have the chance
to snag a hot dog
from the kids'
table, do it! Seize
the moment! Life
is too short!

The Vet

As a general rule, I don't mind going to the vet. Dr. Hexter is chubby (which I respect), is always happy to see me, and always has a big smile. I know my treats are coming soon when he throws open the door to the exam room and bellows, "Well, Hello there!" and gives mom a big hug. Almost like Santa Claus, really. (But he doesn't look like cousin Kyle.)

Coley and me, waiting for Dr. Hexter.

My merriment at the vet all changed the day the ladies behind the big desk decided to give Coley and me nick names. It was an ordinary Saturday morning (I love Saturdays because those are the days Mom gets to stay home with us – all day. And, we don't have to do our morning "let's go potty" in the dark. Sorry, back to my story.) On this Saturday, Mom brought to see Dr. Hexter for our regular arthritis shots (it made our hips feel better) and the friendly, perpetually tan lady behind the desk exclaimed as we walked in, "Oh it's the sweet one! And... the... *other one.*"

I'll give you one guess as to who the "other one" was. So I don't like everyone to pet *me* all the time and I may snap at a finger or two if stuck in my face. I know I'm awesome; I don't need validation of my awesomeness from strangers in the form of superfluous affection. (Good adjective, huh?) I'm fantastic!

So you may be asking now, "Zoe, what's the big deal? It was *one* morning." Oh no, my friend. The name stuck. I was forever known at Dr. Hexter's as "the other one". And, Mom may have told the story to a few hundred people. So word spread. And, it made that year's Christmas card. Do you know how many Christmas cards my Mom sends? Like being in a box with a bow on my head wasn't bad enough! Anyways though, I still like the vet. I'm not one to hold a grudge.

Peace on Earth

Happy Holidays!   Love, Michael, Jennifer, Coley (the sweet one) & Zoe (the other one)

Why Life Isn't Fair

A s I have your attention by now. I hope. I wanted to share my thoughts on things in my life that just aren't fair.

- *I can't have chocolate.* I told Mom I was willing to chance it for one of her peanut butter cup brownies, but she said no.

- *I can't take a cruise.* Not even on Carnival, and you know they let just about anyone on those boats. "Zoe," you may ask, "What's the big deal about you going on a cruise?" Two words, my friend:

midnight buffet.

- *I can't tolerate the heat.* This goes for just about any pug. We are brachiocephalic (Scrabble word! You're welcome!). Our smushed in faces and overall breathing system, coupled with our lack of, well, a snout, means that we can't cool ourselves nearly as well as other dogs. This is a bummer for me because it means I can't sit on Mom's lap while she's floating in the pool. Which means I miss out on a guaranteed opportunity to score some sour cream and onion potato chips and catch up on my chick lit.

- Which brings me to my next point. *I can't read!* Ironic, as I'm able to write this brilliant book. And, as I can't proof read my own book, how do I know Mom didn't change stuff?

- *I age 7-8 times faster than Mom does.* Mom said it's not fair because my life goes by too quickly for *her*, but I'm more concerned that the world needs more time to enjoy *me*.

- *I didn't meet Coley until she was six years old.* According to my calculations (thank you flash cards!), I missed out on anywhere from 36 to… hold on wait…carry the one…42! Yes, 42 dog years of cuddling with her. And cleaning her ears.

- *Michael always gets to pick the TV show.* (See, Mom, I told you I would work that one in here. Where's my bacon, by the way?) The worst is Sports Center. Why are all of the hosts so yelly?

- *I don't have thumbs.* This book would have been sooo much easier to type.

- *Just when I get myself to the perfect scent of an ideal mixture of grass, poop, Milk Bones, and Tide, Mom gives me a shower, and I have to start all over again.*

- *I can't vote.* And with the amount of NPR that Mom listens to, I am very well informed, if not a bit far to the left.

- *I can't talk*, so I can't tell Michael to stop listening to The Grateful Dead. I think I have a better singing voice than that Cherry Garcia guy. Maybe he should have stuck to delicious ice cream? So then Michael told me they were a jam band, and I got really exited. Until he explained it wasn't that kind of jam.

- *Mom works.* A lot. Something about climbing the corporate ladder. Sounds tiring to me. And if she's supposed to practice her climbing, why is she always sitting at her computer?

- *Mom can't explain to me where baby carrots come from.*

- *When I go to the vet, I can't tell Dr. Hexter where it hurts.* So he goes on a multi-orifice exploration.

- *I can't tell Mom how much I love her.* Especially the times she wakes up in the middle of the night to clean up my puke and pulls a mattress down the stairs to sleep on the kitchen floor with me. But, I do cuddle her a lot. So I hope she knows.

I look at Mom with this face, so I think she knows.

Cuddles

Nothing is better than cuddling with your best buddy. Well, except maybe cuddling up with a pound of crispy center-cut bacon. But my Coley and me, we have this cuddling thing down.

In our cozy fleece bed.

On our deck in the warm sunshine.

Sometimes Coley and I get so carried away, we cuddle up right next to each other in the water bowl. Which is the perfect size for two little pug faces, or, one monstrous German Shepherd Dog head. (More dramatic foreshadowing!)

What the Heck is a Cat?

So, Coley and I are enjoying the good life. Then, Mom and Michael decide they want to go to this place called the Humane Society for *another* dog? What?!?!? Um hello, you have the perfect dog, and Coley, here already! What the heck are you doing?

I was relieved when, a few hours later, they came home with no dog! But, they were carrying a cardboard box. And something was making quite a ruckus in it. They pulled out a trembling ball of fur they called a "cat" who proceeded to bolt for Michael's recliner and bury herself *inside* of it. Mom and Michael had to tip over the recliner and dismantle it to get her out. This cat thing then ran for the bathroom and crawled underneath the bottom of the sink. And this was in the first five minutes!

Like the rabbit, this calico cat was beautiful, but looked a bit dumb, so I asked Mom a few questions about her:

Me: *Does she bark?*

Mom: *No, but she may meow from time to time.*

Me: *Weirdo.*

Me: *Does she go outside to the bathroom with us?*

Mom: *No, she goes in a special box inside the house.*

Me: *Wait a minute! We get in trouble when we go in the house. Even when we try to be considerate and aim for the carpet.*

Mom: *It's too dangerous for the cat to go outside. There are coyotes that could scoop her up.*

Me: *What am I? Chopped liver? What if a hawk scoops me up? A turkey vulture tears me to shreds? Or I get strangled by a snake? Trampled by a deer? Chased down by a snapping turtle? Tackled by a gang of squirrels with a score to settle?*

Holly keeping her buddy Coley company after one of Coley's surgeries.

Mom: *Zoe, I think you're being a bit dramatic. And it's just different for cats.*

Me: *Okay, fine. But can I eat her poop?*

Mom: *Off topic and gross, Zoe. And um, no.*

Me: *Okay, does she go outside at all then?*

Mom: *No, she will live her life inside.*

Me: *Fine. Then I'm never going out in the snow ever again. Or wearing that stupid Lands' End orange jacket. With the reflective stripe for safety. And my name embroidered on it. So everyone knows how preppy you are trying to be and how lame I am.*

Mom: *Zoe, I think you're going on a tangent.*

Despite my best efforts to negotiate some special deals with the arrival of my new sister, Holly, she began to live a life even cushier than mine. How was that even possible?

It took Holly a long time to warm up to Mom, Michael, Coley and me. If you consider two years a long time. She seems to favor Coley. And if she's nice to my Coley then, okay, I'll love a cat.

Coley Bear

The "sweet one" is not Coley's only nickname. Mom quickly gave her another rather endearing one – "Coley Bear". You may be asking, "Why bear? Coley is a dog?"

Well, it turns out that Coley didn't really care much for toys when she came to live with us. I don't think she had toys before, so she really didn't know what to do with them. But at the bottom of my (I mean "our") toy box lies a floppy purple teddy bear, who long ago had lost his squeak.

Coley and her bears.

Coley with her other bear. They really love each other. You can see it in their eyes.

Mom calls this Coley's "spare bear". Because, sometimes, even best friends need a break.

Coley immediately decided this little bear would be her new best friend (besides me, of course) and she fell head over paws in love. Since that day, Coley carries the bear everywhere, sometimes in some seemingly uncomfortable positions. Coley cleans him, sleeps with him, and cuddles him. Mom says Coley must be caring for him like he is one of her puppies. Which is sweet really. Even for a puppy hater like me.

I Did NOT Agree to This

"Hey Zoe, do you want to get a puppy?" Mom asked as I tried to settle in for my after-breakfast nap. "Um, nope," I quickly replied. "Come on Zoe, are you sure? Puppies are *really* fun." "Yes, I'm sure. And, no, they are most definitely not." I've been around more than my share of puppies at Grandma Gail's house and I pride myself at the restraint I practice (okay, fine, restraint most of the time) to not bite their little fuzzy, yappy, bobbly heads off.

This better not be our new puppy.

Mom persisted. "You know, Zoe, you can teach a puppy how to do all sorts of stuff, sort of like you did when Coley came, and she didn't know how to play fetch." As I thought about how much fun it was to show Coley how to live a fun life and how having an adoring side kick is quite a boost my own self-esteem, Mom saw my resolve wavering. She went in to seal the deal with, "And Zoe, a puppy would totally look up to you and think you're the greatest." (Crap, Mom's good.)

Here I am with the "puppy".
Friends, do I look happy to you?

About two weeks after our heart to heart, Mom and Michael fed Coley, Holly and me an early supper (no complaints there) and sped off to their friends' Anthony and Carrie's house to pick up our new puppy. When they arrived home two hours later, I was not prepared for what they presented to me as my new little sister. This was no puppy. It was bigger than me! Her huge paws at the ends of its gangly legs were bigger than my head! She was an enormous, black and brown furry monster! She then bounded out of Michael's truck, wild chestnut eyes gleaming in the sun, took one look at me, and tackled me to the ground. When the stars stopped spinning above my cute but startled head, I took one look at Mom and exclaimed in my best Will-Smith-In-Any-Of-His-Cheesy-Movies voice, "Aww, HELL no!"

I spent the next five minutes explaining to Mom (she is very trusting. READ: gullible) why this was a horrible mistake. Clearly Anthony and Carrie sold her a bill of goods, trying to pass this full-grown beast off as a cute little puppy. "She IS a puppy," Mom insisted. "She's a ten-week old German Shepherd Dog! We've named her Jessie! Isn't she the best!?!"

My life would never be the same again.

*Oh, I'm sure you think she looks
all sweet and harmless here.*

68

Eyeballs – Part I

Now, if you are astute, which I imagine you are (as well as good-looking and charming as you are reading this book), you may have noticed in the pictures that my sister Coley went from having two eyeballs to having one eyeball. You, smart, cute and skinny reader, are correct. Mom reminded me that this is a book of short stories, so I'll give you the short version of this one.

Coley and Jessie hanging out, before the accident, when they were still the same size.

It was a few days before Christmas and Mom was home alone baking cookies for a bake sale. She was preparing to run the New York City Half Marathon to raise money for charity and her Christmas Cookie Bake Sale was to be one of her major fund-raisers. After Mom told me that a half marathon was 13.1 miles *in a row* (I try not run on purpose, but you already know about that.), I asked if she could still raise money for charity and take a cab instead. She said it didn't work like that. Sorry, back to my story.

As Mom was busy in the kitchen baking her delicious sugar cookies, Coley had a scuffle while playing with Jessie and in the commotion Jessie accidentally hurt Coley's right eye. It happened in an instant, but, my friend, it was ugly. I saw Coley's eye almost pop out. Like those crazy glasses with the springy eyes, but this was for real. Stunned, Mom quickly gathered her wits about her, assured us it would be okay, and raced Coley to the emergency veterinary hospital. Mom later said it took her 5 minutes to make the 15-minute drive. Upon arrival, Coley was rushed into emergency surgery and Mom was given a hug and handed a box of Kleenex. The nice doctors there could not save Coley's vision in that eye, but they "popped the eyeball back in" (I don't know the medical term for that) and partially stitched up her eyelid so that her newly mobile eyeball would stabilize (i.e., not pop back out). (I know, GROSS! I probably should have given you a disclaimer on this chapter.)

With surgery behind us, the healing began. We didn't know much about eyeballs at the time, but from what Mom could gather from Dr. Hexter, Coley's recovery would be a long and painstaking process. Eyeballs, especially the large and prominent pug kind, are extremely fragile. And when they are injured even the slightest bit of dryness, speck of dust, or accidental bump from a doting sister like me can stop the healing or cause re-injury.

So for the next three weeks Mom spent ALL of her time tending to Coley. She took vacation time for the first few days and then secured permission from her dog-loving boss to work from home so she could keep Coley by her side. Mom administered a detailed regime of eye drops, pain patches, antibiotics, ointments, and codeine like clockwork. She fed Coley chicken and vegetables by hand because Coley no longer wanted to eat on her own. (As pug people know, this is the ultimate sign of trouble.) She gave Coley water through an oral syringe because, most of the time, she was too lethargic to drink. Mom slept on the floor with Coley, because she worried Coley would fall off the bed and she also didn't want her to be alone. Mom set her alarm to buzz through the darkness every two hours so she could wake up throughout the night to keep drops in Coley's eye. Coley needed constant drops because she was no longer blinking or producing her own tears.

Mom and Michael made daily trips to Dr. Hexter (yes, I said daily), to keep trying different methods to help the eye heal, as, during this time, nothing seemed to work for more than a day or two. Add to that, Coley's constant pain. Imagine not being able to blink, or close your eye, EVER, not even to sleep! Coley was way braver than even I, Zoe, would be.

After they exhausted their options, Dr. Hexter sent Coley

to a canine ophthalmologist (yes, there is such a thing) in Fairfield County, CT, a little over an hour from our house. Now my friend, Fairfield County is one of the most expensive places in the country to live. It's a place full of polo clubs and ladies who lunch, where celebrities hide from the bright lights of Hollywood and CEOs escape from the bustle of New York City. So, Mom and Michael knew what this referral would do to my vacation fund. But I agreed that we needed to try anything to help our Coley.

So, on the second day of what would be a sub-zero January, Mom and Michael bundled up Coley and made the one-hour drive to meet the soft-spoken and brilliant Dr. Stuhr. Our kind-hearted Dr. Stuhr was super gentle with Coley, and even gentler with Mom – who was sleep deprived and pretty fragile herself. After some fancy tests he determined that it would be best to remove the eyeball, something called enucleation. Coley had already lost vision in that eye and was in constant pain, so all agreed this was the best choice. Dr. Stuhr would replace the lost eyeball with a rubber prosthesis. (Think bouncy ball out of the gumball machine.) He would then sew it shut so that it looked like Coley had a permanent wink. Cute really. Coley could pull the look off.

Surgery was scheduled for the next day and went off without a hitch! Coley came home from surgery in a bit of a stupor, but stopped trembling for the first time in weeks. I don't know a lot about ophthalmology, but I do know Dr. Stuhr did everything right. Less than 24 hours after surgery, Coley devoured her supper, played with her favorite bear, and cuddled up with me again. And Mom stopped crying.

*Here's Mom and Coley coming home from surgery.
See what I mean by stupor!*

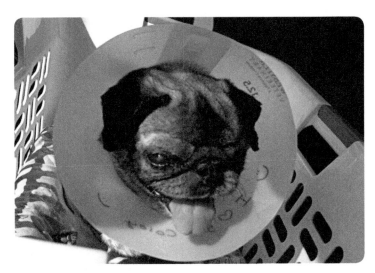

Dr. Stuhr really did give Coley her smile back.

Coley and Jessie. They do love each other.

Coley, her cone, and me hanging out just like always.

So you're probably wondering at this point "Zoe – after all of that, is Coley still friends with Jessie?" And the answer is yes. Coley has always been friends with Jessie, ever since Jessie was a big, dopey, clumsy puppy. Coley doesn't hold grudges. She's the sweet one after all.

The two buddies now, Jessie has 60 more pounds and Coley has one fewer eyeball. But they are both still all smiles!

Why Mom

So my dear reader, you've invested your precious time and energy into reading almost my entire book, but I realize you may have a question lingering in you mind. Why do I call my mom, "Mom," and why do I call my dad, "Michael"? Yet another good question my friend. It's pretty simple really.

Mom and Me. Our younger days.

- Who cleans up after me? Both the not-so-gross and plug-your-nose-and-hold-your-breath gross stuff. Mom.

- Who sleeps on the floor with me when I'm sick? Mom.

- Who drives me pretty much everywhere I want to go. (Including that magical place where they

hand us hot French fries through the car window.)
Mom.

- Who worries herself sick about every eyeball in our
house? Mom.

- Who does my laundry? (You would be surprised
how much laundry a pug can produce.) Mom.

- Who can't cook, but seems to make me the most
delicious suppers? Mom.

- Who can recite and pronounce every medicine I
have taken in my entire life? Like ever. Mom.

- Who wakes me up every so gently when I'm having
a nightmare? Mom.

- Who doesn't get mad when I puke on her bed?
Mom.

- Who saves me from the mean, ugly turkeys who
make themselves way too comfortable in my yard?
Mom.

- Who sings me songs each morning so that I start
my day being happy? Mom.

- Who (besides Coley) is my very best friend? You
guessed it. Mom.

- Who puts herself in a crazy outfit so she can carry
Coley and me outside to go potty in the snow?
Mom.

- Whose idea was it to get a German Shepherd
puppy? Michael's.

That's why Mom.

Aging Gracefully

Friends, I think we know each other pretty well by now. And, by now, you may be wondering about my thoughts on getting older. I am a firm believer in two things – bacon and aging gracefully. Bacon, obvious, but aging gracefully? Here's why.

As I've gotten older, my hearing has gone down the tubes. It happens to the best of us. Over these last several months of writing this book I've progressed to the point of becoming almost completely deaf. Coley, on the other hand, has the ears of a... hmm... you know, someone who can hear really well.

As you know by now, Coley has looked to me to teach her all ways of being a gloriously spoiled dog. And I have happily taken her under my wing. (Okay, paws. Okay, fine, winged paws!) But nowadays our roles are reversing as I depend on her to hear our world. Coley's self-esteem has soared (yes, Mom says dogs have self-esteem) as she serves more and more as my expertly skilled "hearing ear dog." Coley gets to take the lead a lot now, with her head held high and tail bouncing up from between her legs. So my friend, getting older is not so bad, just look at what it's done for Coley and me. Coley gains the self-confidence of a leader and I gain the grace of a follower. It's been a win-win, really.

As you read this heart-warming story you may be asking yourself, "Zoe, that's sweet, do you think Coley really understands that by helping you, she's also helping herself become a happier dog?" I'm sorry, what? Ha, ha, gotcha!!!

An unexpected perk of getting older is being promoted to a front seat bed from my previous back seat crate. Mom says that now that I'm 13, I've earned the right to live a little bit on the edge.

A Good Blanket

I believe that certain blankets have healing properties, for dogs and for humans. Mom has one such magical blanket that she shares with all of us. Our super-powered blanket is the very best kind - fluffy and pink! If you're not feeling well, Mom grabs the pink blanket. If you can't sleep, Mom grabs the pink blanket. If you're sad, you guessed it, Mom grabs the pink blanket. In our house, we know that a good blanket can fix just about anything.

Coley, Jessie and me. If you look closely you can see that Mom's attempt to use the pink blanket as a "German Shepherd drool catcher" failed miserably.

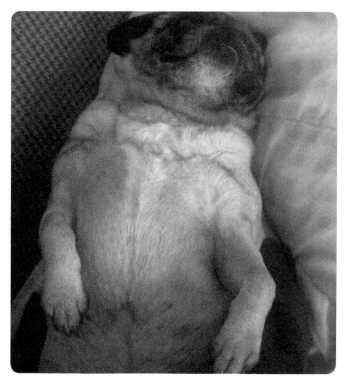

Coley relaxing on the pink blanket after one of her surgeries. She was on pain medicine and out like a light.

Our well-worn pink blanket has been peed on, pooped on, drooled on, sneezed on, and puked on. Mom wanted me to clarify here – all by the dogs. Except maybe the drool. (Mom is a heavy sleeper). But after 17 years and about 500 washings, our pink blanket is still both magical and in one piece. So my friends, find yourself a good blanket - preferably a pink one that smells of the most perfect combination of dog, Tide, and bleach. You'll be sure to thank me.

Grandma Gail and me, hanging out!

Coley again. She's a sucker for the pink blanket ...
... and Mom.

Coley Bear

Ear Wax

There's no delicate way to say this, so I'll come right out with it. Earwax is yummy. Especially Coley's. Especially after a bath. "But Zoe, isn't that gross?" you may ask. Nope, my friend, it's delicious. Don't hold it against me; we all have our vices. I can wax poetic on it for days (sorry, couldn't resist that one). But really, it is quite the delicacy. And besides, I'm saving Mom valuable grooming time. So what if I sometimes leave Coley's ears inside out?

I may or may not have been cleaning Coley's ears right before Mom took this picture of her.

Anyways, Mom frowned upon my suggestion of skipping the Q-tips and employing my talents on *her* ears. I made the case for ear safety. Everyone knows you're not supposed to put Q-tip *in* your ears. But let's be honest, you all do it anyways. And then you look at your Q-tip to see how much gunk you got out before you throw it in the trash. Humans are so gross sometimes. My way would be way better. I bet any otolaryngologist worth his salt would agree. (Yep, I use WebMD.)

Ear cleanings after our baths are especially fun.

Me posing with epicurean delights.
And a stupid sweater. More on that later.

Eyeballs – Part II

This was me on the night in question. I want you to remember, as you read on, how cute, harmless (and festive) I looked.

I'm sure you're thinking to yourself how could such a short book have two chapters on eyeballs. I know. But eyeballs have been a big part of life in my family. This one involved Mom and me. I know what you're thinking and before you go all *Dateline NBC* "Love Betrayed in a Suburban New England Town" with Keith Morrison's creepy voice ringing in your head, let me just throw out two scenarios.

1. It was an accident that I bit Mom in the
    eye.

2. It was dark in the room, I mistook Mom
    for a scary burglar. I became a hero!

As dramatic and exciting as option 2 sounds (I could probably sell a lot more books and maybe get on *Ellen*), the truth lies closer to scenario 1.

Mom said to keep this one short, so here goes.

As you may have guessed by the sparkling tree, this unfortunate eyeball event happened on Christmas night. Mom was home alone with all of us at the time. I know what you're thinking. "Um, hello Zoe, where is Michael when these eyeball things happen?" In his defense, he was at Grandma Gail's helping clean up after the festive spread of beef tenderloin and stuffed lobster tails (I'm still annoyed I wasn't invited).

It was about 9:00 p.m. and Mom, Coley, Jessie and I were getting ready for bed. Jessie was still a (big) puppy. She was 10 months old and about 70 pounds, growing by the minute into full German-Shepherd-Dog muscle, strength and teeth. (I swear sometimes you could just sit there and watch her grow.) I was 10 years old, 18 pounds of aging pug "portliness" and rapidly losing teeth of my own. With this quickly widening disparity between us, I sensed my opportunity to show her who was boss was steadily declining. So on this night, I *may* have tried to pick a fight with her, and she *did* fight back. Neither one of us got hurt, though she did sort of have half of my head in her mouth at one point. We were on the floor when that happened. Mom jumped off the bed to separate us and calm Jessie down. Still riled, I saw my final opening and lunged one last time at my mammoth beast of a sister. I grabbed a piece of skin and chomped down as hard as I could with my jagged little teeth. Ha, ha! I could taste guts! Victory! I looked up to relish my triumph and gaze upon my stunned victim. It was Mom.

Mom dashed out of the room to find towel to wipe the tears flooding down her face. She glanced at herself in the mirror and saw they were not tears though, but rather blood. Mom then raced downstairs to the phone and called Michael. He made the two-mile drive home in about 45 seconds to find a trail of blood following Mom's footsteps throughout the house. (Hey, maybe this story was *Dateline* worthy after all!)

While he assessed the damage Michael stayed calm (he's good at that), quickly put us all to bed and whisked Mom off to the Emergency Room. The doctors examined Mom's eye. It was OK! They couldn't stitch the skin around it because the bite was so ragged. She got a few shots and some pain medicine. There was no need for bandages as her eye had begun to swell shut. In a drug induced haze Mom may have called out "Adrienne!" at one point. But after two hours a happily sedated Mom was sent home. Mom's eye would remain bruised and swollen shut for about three weeks. In my defense, she did get a lot of mileage out of "you should have seen the other guy."

Oh, and of concern to me, is that the hospital was mandated to notify the city of Meriden Dog Warden and report the dog bite. I tried to explain it wasn't like that. They didn't listen. I was officially placed on home quarantine as a dog "potentially dangerous to society". OK, my biting wit, yes, but a canine monster? I don't think so. Have you *seen* what I look like? Either way, I took my sentence with bravery and grit. I was forbidden to leave my property for two weeks. Um, okay, City of Meriden, it's December, you're lucky if I leave the fireplace. Though, I thought, an ankle bracelet could boost my street cred and I quickly requested one. They said it didn't work that way.

Mom and Michael still joke that I have "a record". Which I guess according to the City of Meriden, I do. Mom still has a small scar next to her left eyebrow from one of the deeper parts of her gash. (That must have been a molar). I felt really bad about that. But each time I asked her about it, Mom comforts me with her response, "Zoe, don't worry, every time I look in the mirror for the rest of my life and see my little brown pug-tooth scar, I'll think of you and smile."

My Mom is pretty awesome like that.

Mom, me, and her eyebrow scar!

The Fireplace

Somewhere in the middle of our family room, just to the right of Michael's latest "I-haaaave-to-have-it" flat screen TV, it sits. In the dark of winter, a magical box erupts into glorious, bone-warming flames. It is… da, da, da, da! Our fireplace! With the flick of a button I come running (okay, fine, walking, sort of un-slowly) to the mushy, soft bed that Mom lays in front of just about the most perfect place in the world (next to being face down in a bowl of vanilla cake batter). My fireplace. Sorry Mom, "our" fireplace.

My life in winter.

See, we don't get much "natural warmth" here in Connecticut. For the 10 months out of the year I cannot bask in arthritis-banning sunbeams, I rely on my very best fireplace friend to lull me into a glowing, warm slumber. Michael says if the night is cold enough, he knows where to find the whole family. The five of us (I'm including Mom and her icicle toes).

The German Shepherd Dog knows the pecking order.

can be found in about three square feet of the most prime winter real-estate you'll find north of Palm Coast, Florida. (Where Grandma Gail spends her winters. When I told her pugs don't fly coach, somehow my invite to topical paradise got lost in the mail.) So how I love, our wonderful, magical fireplace!

Honesty

Mom said if I was going to write this book, I had to be honest. So fine, here goes. Here is a chapter of my deepest, darkest confessions. This is a list of animals/people/ others I have bitten over the years. (To the fine folks at Meriden Animal Control – feel free to skip over this chapter.)

Me swimming in a horse's water bucket.

1. A golden retriever named Maggie. In my defense, she was not too bright and "Frosty Paws" were involved. ("Frosty Paws", if you're unfamiliar my friend, is an *ice cream for dogs* and it is delicious!)

2. A rabbit. Fine, my rabbit.

3. A cat. Fine. Two cats. One of them had suspicious eyes and an attitude. Tucker. He had it coming.

4. A horse. On the nose. I left a mark. Mom and I were not invited back to the barn. (On the plus side, I did sneak in a cool dip before we were "asked to leave".)

5. Mom. Yep. You read that chapter too.

6. A German Shepherd Dog. Okay, *my* German Shepherd Dog. We have a long and complicated past. My head has been in *her* mouth, remember?

7. All of my neighbor's dogs. Who were all bigger than me. Except one, my buddy, Scotty. He was huge, looked and sounded like he'd rip you to shreds if you dare enter his domain, but deep down he was a big softy. I even let Mom share my biscuits with him. We finally started keeping some in the mailbox, so that he wouldn't cross his invisible fence line (he got zapped, he didn't care) and plant himself on our front porch.

8. A pug puppy. Fine. Pug *puppies*. Grandma Gail always has litters of pug puppies around. There's only so much of "oh they are the cutest things" that you can take. The puppies want to jump on you and

play with you ALL of the time. And they follow you around like, well, puppies. Ugh!

9. A squirrel. It was actually a very scary *gang* of squirrels. I think from a bad neighborhood. Michael had put my bed outside so I could sleep in the sunshine of a warm fall afternoon. The squirrel gang was nuts! (Sorry, Mom wrote that.) They pounced on me from a ledge on the house, landing square on my back. I bolted into action ready to fight. I didn't actually get any of them, though my reflexes were lightening fast. (Fine, Mom, Honesty chapter, right. I didn't have a chance).

10. A tollbooth operator. Almost. My Mom's reflexes *were* lightening fast. And in my defense, usually if we drive up to a window, they hand us a bag of French fries. So, I was tricked really.

OK, this may seem like a long list, but so that you know I'm not totally evil, here's a list of those I have *not* bitten:

1. Michael. He's always working. And he's kind of tall.

2. My sister Coley. She's a sweetheart, and even if we were just joking around, her self-esteem would never recover.

3. Yonkers Lady. I begged my mom for that one. I'd be like, "Oh hello Yonkers Lady, I'm just a sweet, harmless little pug who will help teach you how to take care of dogs, and then Wham! I'd strike like a police K-9 at a fleeing perp on the lam!" (See Mom, I told you I could work "on the lam" into this

book. I have no idea why that's one of her favorite expressions, and admittedly, hard to work into everyday conversation. Or a book about a dog.) But back to Yonkers Lady – I wouldn't want to end up in doggy jail. (Though the prisoners would probably all say, "What up dog?" That could be funny. But, I already know I can't pull off orange.) Sorry Mom, got off track there.

4. Scotty. (See first list.)

5. Jessie's brother and littermate Damian. Don't let the name fool you. This dog is a 95-pound goofball who will open the front door and lead you straight to the good jewelry and cook you up a steak while you pillage. And besides, Damian belongs to my favorite Aunt Fran. I love her. She buys me Christmas presents, but you already know that. Now that I think more about it, Aunt Fran is a nurse, so, hypothetically, if I were to bite Damian, she could expertly tend to any blood and guts inflicted by my jaws of death. Oh wait, Mom just reminded me, Aunt Fran is a nurse in a *colonoscopy* clinic. Yep, I'll leave Damian alone.

Am I proud of this seemingly lopsided 2:1 ratio? Yep! I'm also proud that I know what a ratio is. The time that my Mom and I spent on the flashcards is really paying off!

In closing, my friend, I submit to you Exhibit A. Jessie is on the left. Her brother Damian is on the right. So, I like to think this makes me even in the world of German Shepherd Dogs.

*Jesse and Damian, loving
life on a warm summer day.*

So Not Funny

So, it's about one week after Coley had her eyeball removed (or enucleated – which just sounds gross). I'm sitting by Mom's feet thinking about what Dr. Stuhr did with her actual eyeball after replacing it with the prosthetic (thanks spell check). Does Dr. Stuhr have a jar of dog eyeballs to freak out the neighborhood kids on Halloween? Does he donate them to science? Does Coley gets a donor sticker on her dog license?

Our one-eyed wonder.

Sorry, back to my story. Mom and Michael are having some conversation about how Mom think's Coley's new bionic rubber eyeball is shifting around in its freshly sutured socket. She is working herself into an impressive panic. *Is Coley OK? Is she in pain? Is the rubber ball going to somehow burst through three layers of stitches and bounce down the hallway?* It's a Sunday, and Michael said this is not a "medical emergency" worthy of calling Dr. Stuhr at this moment, so after 45 minutes of pretty logical responses to Mom's illogical line of questioning, Michael promises to call Dr. Stuhr first thing Monday morning.

Sweet Coley in her fall jacket. I had ripped mine off.

Fast forward to Monday evening, after Michael had spoken with Dr. Stuhr. When Mom came home from work, he relayed what Dr. Stuhr explained. "Don't worry, sometimes the socket rejects the new fake eyeball. Sometimes the stitches loosen. Sometimes they break. Sometimes, in rare cases, the rubber eyeball does pop out. But it's not a big deal, just catch it, rinse it off, and pop it back in."

Mom's face dropped in terror. She uttered a series of words which I pinky swore not to repeat. (Well, I would have pinky swore, if I had a pinky.) But Michael kept going, adding to and intensifying this horrific story. As Mom began to feel faint, he saw it was time to stop. Michael explained, "Dr. Stuhr said it's fine. The layers of stitches are more than secure. It may shift a tiny bit in the socket while it's settling in, but that teensy change is so small it's virtually imperceptible." (Well, imperceptible to anyone other than mom.) Michael then chuckled as he went on to explain what Dr. Stuhr added to his explanation – "But I know Jen is wound a bit tight around Coley and these surgeries, so please, have a bit of fun with this one."

So not funny.

Clothes

DOGS SHOULD NOT WEAR CLOTHES. Okay, wait; dogs should wear clothes for MEDICAL REASONS ONLY. See, I had to wear a shirt for a while because the steroid medicine Mom gave me to help my breathing gave me unsightly bumps all over my skin. Actually, the "shirt" was a baby onesie. Yep, you read that right. A "6-9 months" is the perfect size for a chubby senior pug. (Thanks for THAT recommendation Dr. Hexter!) When Mom came home with that fateful bag from Target I quickly learned that I had the choice between pink hearts and purple bows. Really, Mom? You couldn't find a nice slimming vertical stripe?

Do I look like I'm happy here?!?

Dr. Hexter had to shave my fur surrounding my bumps so they could get the medicine directly on my skin. Stupid fur. I know he was trying to make it better, but I looked like a hot mess. (Yep, Mom lets me watch Wendy Williams.) Well, anyways, I left the bumps alone so they could heal. I'm smart. I'm not a cone kind of dog. (In 13 years, I've never spent one day in a cone. I'm proud of that.)

The culprit. And her accomplice.

So, my friend, I know what you're going to ask. "If you left your skin bumps alone so that they could heal, why did you have to wear a onesie?" Two words: Nurse Coley. See,

Coley thought she could "speed along" the healing process by cleaning my bumps herself. She's the "sweet one" after all; she was trying to help. Between you and me, I think she may have just liked that my skin naturally emanates an aroma very similar to Canadian bacon. Coley couldn't WAIT for Mom to leave for work; she'd yank off my onesie and go to town on my back before Mom even made it out of the driveway. This would not have been a problem if Mom could button the bottom of the onesie closed. But, Mom couldn't secure the bottom closed because, well, um, small detail, but, BABIES DON'T HAVE TAILS!

I tried to tell Mom what was going on, but she didn't believe me. Her sweet Coley would *never* cause a bother. But then Mom came home from work early one Thursday and found me sitting there, with the onesie over my head. I left it that way *all day*. It was uncomfortable, and I got kind of hot, but I didn't care. I needed hard evidence. Oh, and yes, before you ask, the picture of me in a pink polka dot onesie (with *sleeves*) made THAT year's Christmas card. But don't worry, I'm good.

A strong sense of self comes in handy sometimes.

*Nothing like an afternoon nap
at our cottage in Maine.*

Sleep

Mom told me once that often times humans have a hard time sleeping. Sometimes, they actually have to take medicine to help them sleep! What! That's awful; I couldn't believe my velvety button ears! Now, I'm not perfect (See, this is my attempt at modesty. I know you're seeing right through it.), but one thing I can do is sleep. Next to food, sleep is just about the most wonderful thing ever. My friend, you should never be afraid of taking a good snooze – whenever, wherever, and however you can.

Pug butt to pug butt.

About the Other Author

Jennifer Niland Wright spent almost 20 years writing for one of the largest healthcare insurance companies in the world, but it only took one five-ounce pug puppy named Zoe to awaken her creative side. Jennifer is quite sure there must be someone somewhere in the world who really WANTS to write about insurance, to climb the corporate ladder, and to maintain a very comfortable living, but after she saw Zoe grow old before her eyes, Jennifer realized it was no longer she.

She wanted to write about Zoe. She wanted to write about all the Zoes in the world, innocent little creatures who grow up with their own distinct personalities, little creatures who are at first pets, but then become very real children.

"No more insurance!" Zoe demanded. "We want a stay-at-home dog mom!"

So Jennifer quit! And she started writing about life with Zoe, about all the warmth and affection and love the pug had to offer, but also about Zoe's shortcomings that could make her such a, well, pill. Jennifer's other pets started sauntering into her writing as well: more spoiled pugs, a ball crazy German Shepherd Dog, a neurotic calico cat, a fickle lop eared rabbit, and one endlessly patient husband.

With buttoned-up corporate culture firmly behind her, Jennifer and her husband left their native Connecticut and moved to a quiet coastal town in Northeast Florida where she continues to write and photograph the adventures of her furry gang of misfits. You are most welcome to visit her at JenniferNilandWright.com.

CPSIA information can be obtained
at www.ICGtesting.com
Printed in the USA
BVOW11*2129260517

484585BV00002B/2/P